Planning

for Learning

through

nursery

rhymes

Rachel Sparks Linfield

Illustrated by Cathy Hughes

Contents

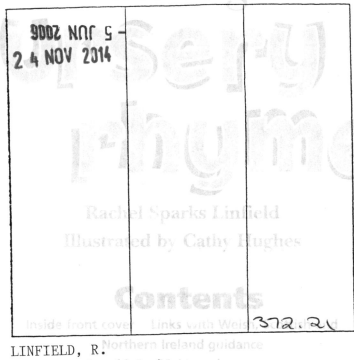

Published by Step Forward Publishing Limited
25 Cross Street, Leamington Spa, CV32 4PX   Tel: 01926 420046   www.practicalpreschool.com
© Step Forward Publishing Limited 2001

Planning for Learning through Nursery Rhymes   ISBN: 1-902438-30-2

MAKING PLANS

WHY PLAN?

The purpose of planning is to make sure that all children enjoy a broad and balanced curriculum. All planning should be useful. Plans are working documents which you spend time preparing, but which should later repay your efforts. Try to be concise. This will help you in finding information quickly when you need it.

LONG-TERM PLANS

Preparing a long-term plan, which maps out the curriculum during a year or even two, will help you to ensure that you are providing a variety of activities and are meeting the statutory requirements of the Early Learning Goals.

Your long-term plan need not be detailed. Divide the time period over which you are planning into fairly equal sections, such as half terms. Choose a topic for each section. Young children benefit from making links between the new ideas they encounter, so as you select each topic, think about the time of year in which you plan to do it. A topic about minibeasts will not be very successful in November!

Although each topic will address all the learning areas, some could focus on a specific area. For example, a topic on Nursery Rhymes lends itself well to activities relating to Personal, Social and Emotional Development and Communication, Language and Literacy. Another topic might particularly encourage children to investigate, to observe and to ask questions. Try to make sure that you provide a variety of topics in your long-term plans.

Autumn 1	Nursery rhymes
Autumn 2	Autumn/Christmas
Spring 1	All about me
Spring 2	Colour
Summer 1	Toys
Summer 2	Minibeasts

MEDIUM-TERM PLANS

Medium-term plans will outline the contents of a topic in a little more detail. One way to start this process is by brainstorming on a large piece of paper. Work with your team writing down all the activities you can think of which are relevant to the topic. As you do this, it may become clear that some activities go well together.

Think about dividing them into themes. The topic of Nursery Rhymes, for example, has themes such as 'Humpty Dumpty', 'Jack and Jill' and 'Little Miss Muffet'.

At this stage, it is helpful to make a chart. Write the theme ideas down the side of the chart and put a different area of learning at the top of each column. Now you can insert your brainstormed ideas and will quickly see where there are gaps. As you complete the chart, take account of children's earlier experiences and provide opportunities for them to progress.

Refer back to the Early Learning Goals document and check that you have addressed as many different aspects of it as you can. Once all your medium-term plans are complete, make sure that there are no neglected areas.

DAY-TO-DAY PLANS

The plans you make for each day will outline aspects such as:

MAKING PLANS

- resources needed;
- the way in which you might introduce activities;
- the organisation of adult help;
- size of the group;
- timing.

Identify the learning which each activity is intended to promote. Make a note of any assessments or observations which you are likely to carry out. On your plans, make notes of which activities were particularly successful, or any changes you would make another time.

A FINAL NOTE

Planning should be seen as flexible. Not all groups meet every day, and not all children attend every day. Any part of the plan can be used independently, stretched over a longer period or condensed to meet the needs of any group. You will almost certainly adapt the activities as children respond to them in different ways and bring their own ideas, interests and enthusiasms. The important thing is to ensure that the children are provided with a varied and enjoyable curriculum which meets their individual developing needs.

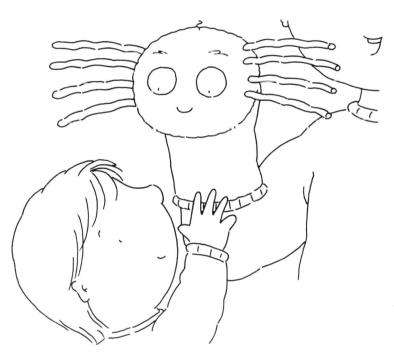

USING THE BOOK

- Collect or prepare suggested resources as listed on page 21.
- Read the section which outlines links to the Early Learning Goals document (pages 4 - 7) and explains the rationale for the topic of Nursery Rhymes.
- For each weekly theme, two activities are described in detail as examples to help you in your planning and preparation. Key vocabulary, questions and learning opportunities are identified.
- The skills chart on page 23 will help you to see at a glance which aspects of children's

development are being addressed as a focus each week.

- As children take part in the Nursery Rhymes topic activities, their learning will progress. 'Collecting evidence' on page 22 explains how you might monitor children's achievements.
- Find out on page 20 how the topic can be brought together in a grand finale involving parents, children and friends.
- There is additional material to support the working partnership of families and children in the form of a 'Home links' page, and a photocopiable 'Parent's page' found at the back of the book.

It is important to appreciate that the ideas presented in this book will only be a part of your planning. Many activities which will be taking place as routine in your group may not be mentioned. For example, it is assumed that sand, dough, water, puzzles, floor toys and large scale apparatus are part of the ongoing Foundation Stage experience, as are the opportunities which increasing numbers of groups are able to offer for children to develop ICT skills. Role-play areas, stories, rhymes and singing, and group discussion times are similarly assumed to be happening in each week although they may not be a focus for described activities.

USING THE EARLY LEARNING GOALS

Having decided on your topic and made your medium-term plans, you can use the Early Learning Goals to highlight the key learning opportunities your activities will address. The goals are split into six areas: Personal, Social and Emotional Development; Communication, Language and Literacy; Mathematical Development; Knowledge and Understanding of the World; Physical Development and Creative Development. Do not expect each of your topics to cover every goal but your long-term plans should allow for all of them to be addressed by the time a child enters Year 1.

The following section highlights parts of the Early Learning Goals document in point form to show what children are expected to be able to do by the time they enter Year 1 in each area of learning. These points will be used throughout this book to show how activities for a topic on Nursery Rhymes link to these expectations. For example, Personal, Social and Emotional Development point 9 is 'understand what is right, what is wrong and why'. Activities suggested which provide the opportunity for children to do this will have the reference PS9. This will enable you to see which parts of the Early Learning Goals are covered in a given week and plan for areas to be revisited and developed.

In addition, you can ensure that activities offer variety in the goals to be encountered. Often, a similar activity may be carried out to achieve different learning objectives. For example, when children make 'Lost sheep' posters for Little Bo Peep in Week 6, they will be learning about writing for different purposes whilst at the same time using their imagination in art. It is important, therefore, that activities have clearly defined goals so that these may be emphasised during the activity and for recording purposes.

PERSONAL, SOCIAL AND EMOTIONAL DEVELOPMENT (PS)

This area of learning covers important aspects of development which affect the way children learn, behave and relate to others.

By the end of the Foundation Stage, most children will:

PS1   continue to be interested, excited and motivated to learn

PS2   be confident to try activities, initiate ideas and speak in a familiar group

PS3   maintain attention, concentrate and sit quietly when appropriate

PS4   have a developing awareness of their own needs, views and feelings and be sensitive to the needs, views and feelings of others

PS5   have a developing respect for their own cultures and beliefs and those of other people

PS6   respond to significant experiences, showing a range of feelings when appropriate

PS7   form good relationships with adults and peers

PS8   work as a part of a group or class, taking turns and sharing fairly, understanding that there need to be agreed values and codes of behaviour for groups of people, including adults and children, to work together harmoniously

PS9   understand what is right, what is wrong and why

PS10   dress and undress independently and manage their own personal hygiene

PS11   select and use activities and resources independently

PS12   consider the consequences of their words and actions for themselves and others

PS13   understand that people have different needs, views, cultures and beliefs, that need to be treated with respect

PS14   understand that they can expect others to treat their needs, views, cultures and beliefs with respect

The topic of Nursery Rhymes offers many opportunities for children's personal and social development. Time spent discussing why Miss Muffet was frightened by the spider and how it feels to break something, like Humpty Dumpty, will encourage children to speak in a group, to be interested and to consider consequences. By playing circle games, children will learn to take turns and to understand the need for agreed codes of behaviour. Many of the areas outlined above, though, will be covered on an almost incidental basis as children carry out the activities described in this book for the other areas of children's learning. During undirected free choice times, they will be developing PS11 whilst any small group activity which involves working with an adult will help children to work towards PS7.

COMMUNICATION, LANGUAGE AND LITERACY (L)

The objectives set out in the *National Literacy Strategy: Framework for Teaching* for the reception year are in line with these goals. By the end of the Foundation Stage, most children will be able to:

L1 enjoy listening to and using spoken and written language, and readily turn to it in their play and learning

L2 explore and experiment with sounds, words and texts

L3 listen with enjoyment, and respond to stories, songs and other music, rhymes and poems and make up their own stories, songs, rhymes and poems

L4 use language to imagine and recreate roles and experiences

L5 use talk to organise, sequence and clarify thinking, ideas, feelings and events

L6 sustain attentive listening, responding to what they have heard by relevant comments, questions or actions;

L7 interact with others, negotiating plans and activities and taking turns in conversation

L8 extend their vocabulary, exploring the meaning and sounds of new words

L9 retell narratives in the correct sequence, drawing on language patterns of stories

L10 speak clearly and audibly with confidence and control and show awareness of the listener, for example by their use of conventions such as greetings, 'please' and 'thank you'

L11 hear and say initial and final sounds in words, and short vowel sounds within words

L12 link sounds to letters, naming and sounding letters of the alphabet

L13 read a range of familiar and common words and simple sentences independently

L14 show an understanding of the elements of stories such as main character, sequence of events, and openings, and how information can be found in non-fiction texts to answer questions about where, who, why and how

L15 know that print carries meaning and, in English, is read from left to right and top to bottom

L16 attempt writing for different purposes, using features of different forms such as lists, stories and instructions

L17 write their own names and other things such as labels and captions, and begin to form simple sentences, sometimes using punctuation

L18 use their phonic knowledge to write simple regular words and make phonetically plausible attempts at more complex words

L19 use a pencil and hold it effectively to form recognisable letters, most of which are correctly formed

Nursery rhymes provide a rich resource for activities that help children to develop a sense of rhyme. Some of the activities suggested encourage children to use their imaginations as they enjoy listening to the rhymes and to respond in a variety of ways to what they hear, reinforcing and extending their vocabularies. Throughout the topic, opportunities are described in which children are encouraged to explore the sounds of words, to use descriptive vocabulary, to identify initial sounds and to see some of their ideas recorded in both pictures and words.

MATHEMATICAL DEVELOPMENT (M)

The key objectives in the *National Numeracy Strategy: Framework for Teaching* for the reception year are in line with these goals. By the end of the Foundation Stage, most children will be able to:

M1 say and use number names in order in familiar contexts

M2 count reliably up to ten everyday objects

 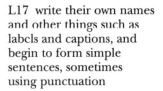

M3 recognise numerals 1 to 9

M4 use language such as 'more' or 'less' to compare two numbers

M5 in practical activities and discussion begin to use the vocabulary involved in adding and subtracting

M6 find one more or one less than a number from one to ten.

M7 begin to relate addition to combining two groups of objects and subtraction to 'taking away'

M8 talk about, recognise and recreate simple patterns

M9 use language such as 'circle' or 'bigger' to describe the shape and size of solids and flat shapes

M10 use everyday words to describe position

M11 use developing mathematical ideas and methods to solve practical problems

M12 use language such as 'greater', 'smaller', 'heavier' or 'lighter' to compare quantities

The theme of Nursery Rhymes provides a meaningful context for mathematical activities. Children are given the opportunity to count Little Bo Peep's sheep and the bricks in Humpty Dumpty's wall and to begin to develop language for addition and subtraction. There are opportunities for children to play a variety of number games and to enjoy using counting rhymes based on the nursery rhymes. Rhymes such as 'Jack and Jill' and 'The Grand Old Duke of York' are an excellent stimulus for activities to encourage the use of positional language.

KNOWLEDGE AND UNDERSTANDING OF THE WORLD (K)

By the end of the Foundation Stage, most children will be able to:

K1 investigate objects and materials by using all of their senses as appropriate

K2 find out about, and identify, some features of living things, objects and events they observe

K3 look closely at similarities, differences, patterns and change

K4 ask questions about why things happen and how things work

K5 build and construct with a wide range of objects, selecting appropriate resources and adapting their work where necessary

K6 select the tools and techniques they need to shape, assemble and join materials they are using

K7 find out about and identify the uses of everyday technology and use information and communication technology and programmable toys to support their learning

K8 find out about past and present events in their own lives, and in those of their families and other people they know

K9 observe, find out about and identify features in the place they live and the natural world

K10 begin to know about their own cultures and beliefs and those of other people

K11 find out about their environment and talk about those features they like and dislike

The topic of Nursery Rhymes offers many opportunities for children to make observations, to ask questions and to compare. They can consider why Humpty Dumpty broke and which materials can be dropped safely. By investigating ways to stop cotton wool spiders from sticking on a tape web and making magnetic mice, they will become more aware of the properties of materials. Activities which involve looking for spiders' webs and observing items made from wool will encourage children to gain a greater understanding of their local environment.

PHYSICAL DEVELOPMENT (PD)

By the end of the Foundation Stage, most children will be able to:

PD1 move with confidence, imagination and in safety

PD2 move with control and coordination

PD3 show awareness of space, of themselves and of others

PD4 recognise the importance of keeping healthy and those things which contribute to this

PD5 recognise the changes that happen to their bodies when they are active

PD6 use a range of small and large equipment

PD7 travel around, under, over and through balancing and climbing equipment

PD8 handle tools, objects, construction and malleable materials safely and with increasing control

Activities such as playing with dough and construction toys with small pieces will offer experience of PD8. Through pretending to be Miss Muffet's spider, a sheep dog looking for Little Bo Peep's sheep or the Grand Old Duke of York, children will have the opportunity to develop PD1 and 2. A variety of activities encourage children to aim, balance and climb.

CREATIVE DEVELOPMENT (C)

By the end of the Foundation Stage most children will be able to:

C1 explore colour, texture, shape, form and space in two or three dimensions

C2 recognise and explore how sounds can be changed, sing simple songs from memory, recognise repeated sounds and sound patterns and match movements to music

C3 respond in a variety of ways to what they see, hear, smell, touch and feel

C4 use their imagination in art and design, music, dance, imaginative and role play and stories

C5 express and communicate their ideas, thoughts and feelings by using a widening range of materials, suitable tools, imaginative and role play, movement, designing and making, and a variety of songs and musical instruments

During this topic, children will experience working with a variety of materials as they make collages, models and puppets. They will be able to develop their skills of painting and colour mixing as they paint self portraits and pictures of nursery rhyme characters and work towards C1 and 4. Actions and percussion

are encouraged for a number of nursery rhymes so allowing children to use their imaginations in music. Throughout all the activities, children are encouraged to talk about what they see and feel as they communicate their ideas in painting, collage work and role play.

Week 1
HUMPTY DUMPTY

PERSONAL, SOCIAL AND EMOTIONAL DEVELOPMENT

- During circle time, talk about feelings children have when something is broken (see activity opposite). (PS2, 3, 6)

- Read *Little Lumpty* by Miko Imai (Walker Books). Little Lumpty disobeys his mother when he climbs the wall that Humpty Dumpty fell from. Talk about what Little Lumpty did. What made him decide to climb the wall? (PS9, 12)

- 'All the king's horses and all the king's men, Couldn't put Humpty together again'. As a group, brainstorm ideas for how the king's men could mend Humpty Dumpty. (PS2, 8)

COMMUNICATION, LANGUAGE AND LITERACY

- Enjoy making new names for Humpty Dumpty by changing the initial letters (see activity opposite). (L2, 11, 17)

- Provide each child with a picture of Humpty Dumpty sitting on a large brick wall. Encourage children to use the wall to practise down strokes as they fill the bricks with brightly coloured vertical lines. (L19)

- Begin a word bank of words which rhyme with 'wall'. Help children to realise that by changing the initial sound the word changes. Write the words suggested by children on pairs of cards and use them to play pelmanism and other matching games. (L11, 13)

MATHEMATICAL DEVELOPMENT

- Use egg cupfuls of water to estimate, to measure and to compare the capacity of a variety of plastic containers. (M12)

- Use a range of construction toys, multi-link cubes, empty boxes, and so on, to make walls for Humpty Dumpty to sit on. Count the number of bricks in each wall. Compare the heights of the walls and arrange them in order of height. (M4, 12)

- Provide each child with a wall drawn on A4 sized card where a number has been written on each brick. In turn, children shake a die and cover up the brick which matches the number thrown. If no brick shows the thrown number, the turn is missed. The winner is the first player to cover all their bricks. (M3)

KNOWLEDGE AND UNDERSTANDING OF THE WORLD

- Humpty Dumpty was shaped like an egg. Use picture books to find out information about animals which hatch from eggs. (K2, 4)

- Grow cress in washed, half egg-shells on soaked kitchen towel. Observe the cress each day and make sure that the kitchen towel is always kept damp. Once the cress has grown, decorate the egg-shells with felt-pens to turn them into Humpty Dumpty egg heads. (K3)

- Humpty Dumpty broke when he fell. Ask children to suggest what sorts of materials break when they are dropped. Make a collection of objects which do not break when dropped such as a ball, a teddy bear and a plastic cup. Ask children to examine the objects and to think of reasons why they can be dropped safely. (K3, 4)

PHYSICAL DEVELOPMENT

- Humpty Dumpty hurt himself when he fell from the wall. Talk about the need to bend knees when jumping and how to land safely. Enjoy practising jumping. Encourage children to make short and long jumps, high and low ones, quick and slow jumps. (PD1, 2, 4)

- Use malleable materials to make models of Humpty Dumpty. (PD8)

- Use climbing equipment to enjoy pretending to climb walls. (PD7)

CREATIVE DEVELOPMENT

- Provide each child with a Humpty Dumpty shape cut from a piece of A3 sized card. Encourage the children to use a variety of fabrics and papers to turn the shape into a Humpty Dumpty. (C1, 4)

- Invite children to make a wall from cereal boxes which have been turned inside out and painted. Display the Humpty Dumpty collages on the wall. (C1)

- Set up the role-play area as a doctor's surgery for nursery rhyme characters. In the waiting area, put out a range of nursery rhyme books. Ask children to suggest ideas for which characters might need to make a visit. Encourage them to visit the surgery in role as a nursery rhyme character. (C5)

ACTIVITY: Circle time about breaking something

Learning opportunity: Talking with confidence about feelings.

Early Learning Goal: Personal, Social and Emotional Development. Children will be confident to initiate ideas and to speak. They will show feelings.

Resources: A broken toy in a box.

Key vocabulary: Broken, break, mend, feel.

Organisation: Whole group sitting comfortably in a circle.

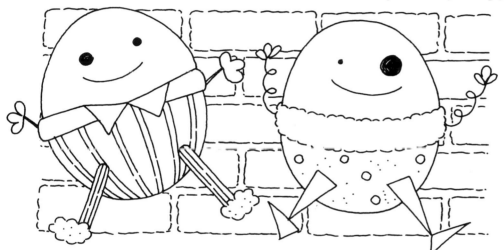

WHAT TO DO:

Circle time should be a positive time. The purpose of this activity is not to apportion blame. Care must be taken to avoid this happening - the emphasis should be on the importance of caring for toys and treating them properly.

Show children the box which contains the broken toy. Shake the box and ask children to listen to the sounds they hear. Can they guess what is in the box? Remove one piece of the broken toy and show it to the group. What is it? What has it come from? Show the group all the pieces. Explain that they used to be a toy which children enjoyed playing with but now it is broken. How do children think that the toy was broken? Could it be mended? Finish by inviting children to talk about their feelings when they break something.

ACTIVITY: Making new names for Humpty Dumpty

Learning opportunity: Experimenting with rhyming words.

Early Learning Goal: Communication, Language and Literacy. Children will explore and experiment with words, hear and say initial sounds and write labels.

Resources: Large strips of card with the words 'umpty umpty' written on them; thick-tipped felt-pen; area for displaying the name cards; large poster of the alphabet or cards with the letters written on; a big book version of Humpty Dumpty.

Key vocabulary: Humpty Dumpty, beginning, start.

Organisation: Whole group sitting comfortably on the floor for the introduction. Small groups at tables for the written activity.

WHAT TO DO:

Begin by looking at a big book version of 'Humpty Dumpty' and enjoy reciting the nursery rhyme, as a group, at a variety of speeds. Explain to the group that they are going to make a new rhyme by changing Humpty Dumpty's name. Show children the B alphabet card. Ask them what Humpty Dumpty's name would be if it began with the 'b' sound. Fill in the letters on a name strip to show Bumpty Dumpty. Encourage children to suggest other rhyming names and scribe these on name strips. Break into smaller groups and provide each child with an A4 piece of paper on which '_umpty _umpty' is written. Invite children to make their own new name and to draw a picture of their new nursery rhyme character.

DISPLAY

Display the Humpty Dumpty collages on the cereal packet brick wall. Invite children to choose a name which rhymes with Humpty Dumpty to be placed near their collage. On a large piece of paper, write out the nursery rhyme and mount it near the display. Encourage children to read the name labels and to count the number of bricks in the wall and the Humpty Dumpties.

Week 2
LITTLE MISS MUFFET

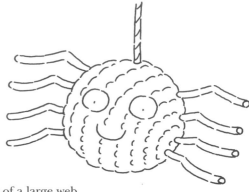

PERSONAL, SOCIAL AND EMOTIONAL DEVELOPMENT

- Little Miss Muffet is scared of spiders. Discuss other things which Miss Muffet might be frightened of. Invite the children to draw pictures of things which frighten either Miss Muffet or them and display these in a large web. (PS2, 8)

- During a circle time, talk sensitively about things which scare people but which, when explained, are not frightening such as shadows, noises and spiders. (PS4, 6)

- Although we are often frightened of minibeasts such as spiders, wasps and caterpillars, we are giants compared with them. Talk to children about the need to take care of minibeasts. Go outside to look for spiders and to admire their webs. (PS1, 9)

COMMUNICATION, LANGUAGE AND LITERACY

- 'Little Miss Muffet, sat on a tuffet'. Help the children to write rhyming couplets for new characters and places to sit such as 'Little Miss Cool, sat on a stool' and 'Tall Doctor Cable, sat under a table'. (L8, 18)

- Read *Dear Bear* by Joanna Harrison (Collins Picture Lions). In the story, Katie overcomes her fear of 'the bear under the stairs'. Help children to write or draw letters for Miss Muffet's spider (see activity opposite). (L6, 16)

- Enjoy rhymes and stories with spider connections such as 'Incy Wincy Spider'. Encourage children to join in with the actions. (L3)

MATHEMATICAL DEVELOPMENT

- Make spiders from black pompons and pipe-cleaners. Encourage children to count the legs. Attach elastic to each spider and hang them around the room. (M2)

- Use pictures of spiders and plastic toy spiders to help children realise that all spiders have eight legs. Provide each child with a drawing of a spider body and a die with the numbers one, two and three on it. In turn, children shake the die and add that number of legs. The first person to give their spider eight legs is the winner. (M2, 3)

- Use thin, black felt-pens to draw straight lines on large card hexagons to make spiders' webs. Talk to children about the number of sides on the hexagon shapes and encourage them to help in the making of a large web and to notice how the hexagons will fit together. (M9)

KNOWLEDGE AND UNDERSTANDING OF THE WORLD

- Discuss why spiders spin webs. Use non-fiction books to make a collection of facts about webs. For example, spiders make new webs each day and the web is a store for food. (K2, 9)

- Spiders' feet are covered with a special oil which prevents them from sticking to their webs. Investigate what stops a cotton wool ball from sticking to double-sided sticky tape (see activity opposite). (K1, 2, 3)

- Go on a web hunt. Identify the places where spiders like to make their webs. Do spiders like dark corners? Do they need special areas to start their webs or can they spin them on a smooth wall? (K9)

PHYSICAL DEVELOPMENT

- Use the 'Little Miss Muffet' nursery rhyme as the stimulus for imaginative movement. Recite the rhyme several times encouraging children to mime to the words. Change the 'sat down beside her' line to include a variety of movements such as 'jumped down', 'tiptoed' and 'skipped'. Encourage children to listen carefully to the rhyme and to move in time with the words. (PD1, 2, 3)

- Use playground chalk to draw a large web outside. Encourage children to move around the web lines using a variety of movements. (PD1, 2, 3)

- Tell the story of a spider which wakes up early, spins its web and goes out to visit Miss Muffet. Encourage children to be spiders and to mime to the story. (PD1)

CREATIVE DEVELOPMENT

- Make sparkly webs by painting web patterns with watered-down PVA glue on black sugar paper and then sprinkling silver glitter on top. (C1)

- Use paper plates and card to make large spider puppets. Attach a piece of dowelling to the back with sticky tape (see diagram). Use the puppets to tell the story of Miss Muffet. (C1, 4)

- Paint portraits of Miss Muffet. (C4)

ACTIVITY: Writing letters to Miss Muffet's spider

Learning opportunity: Listening attentively with imagination and writing letters to Miss Muffet's spider.

Early Learning Goal: Communication, Language and Literacy. Children will sustain attentive listening and attempt writing.

Resources: *Dear Bear* by Joanna Harrison (Collins Picture Lions); variety of papers, crayons, pens and pencils.

Key vocabulary: Dear, from, spider.

Organisation: Whole group sitting comfortably on the floor for the introduction. Small groups at tables for the written activity.

WHAT TO DO:

Read *Dear Bear* by Joanna Harrison (Collins Picture Lions). Talk about Katie and her fear of the bear under the stairs. Look at the pictures of Katie and the bear. Ask children why Katie grew to like the bear and why she worried when she thought he might be ill.

Recite the Miss Muffet nursery rhyme. Talk about why Miss Muffet ran away. Suggest to the children that if Miss Muffet had made friends with the spider, she might not have needed to run away.

Show children the paper and ask them to help Miss Muffet to make letters for the spider. What might she want to say in her letter? In small groups, help children to write/draw letters for the spider. Make a class book of 'Dear Spider' letters.

ACTIVITY: Investigating sticky webs

Learning opportunity: Observing and noticing similarities and differences.

Early Learning Goal: Knowledge and Understanding of the World. Children will investigate materials using their senses. They will identify features of objects they observe and look closely at similarities and differences.

Resources: Double-sided sticky tape; cotton wool balls; hand cream; washing-up liquid; cooking oil; large piece of paper; table cover; picture of a spider in a web.

Key vocabulary: Spider, web, sticky, oily, feet.

Organisation: Small group.

WHAT TO DO:

Show children the picture of the web and talk about the way spiders use webs to catch minibeasts. Ask why a fly which lands on the web is caught. Next, ask why they think a spider can walk in its own web without being caught. Explain that a spider's feet are covered with a special oil which stops them from sticking. Show the group a piece of double-sided tape stuck across an A4 piece of stiff card and the cotton wool balls. Ask the group to imagine that each cotton wool ball is a spider and that the tape is a web. What do they think will happen if a 'spider' is placed on the 'web'? Place a cotton wool ball on the tape, turn the card upside down and show how easily it sticks. Show the group the washing-up liquid, the hand cream and the oil. Dip a 'spider' in the oil and place it on the tape. Watch how easily the 'spider' now slips from the 'web'. Repeat with the washing-up liquid and the hand cream. Discuss with the children what they would cover their feet with if they were spiders and why.

DISPLAY

Display the hexagonal webs as a giant patchwork and hang some of the pompon spiders from it. Make a large web with white string and suspend the rest of the spiders from this. Mount the portraits of Miss Muffet and display these nearby. On a table put out a large teddy bear, the book *Dear Bear* and a class book of the children's 'Dear Spider' letters.

Week 3
JACK AND JILL

PERSONAL, SOCIAL AND EMOTIONAL DEVELOPMENT

- Jack and Jill went to collect water. Talk about the importance of water and the many ways in which water is used. (PS2, 3, 4)

- During a circle time, talk about ways to help someone who falls down. Role play being Jack and Jill and helping each other after the fall. (PS3, 7)

- Jack and Jill had to carry a pail of water. Talk about the way they would have carried it so that the water did not spill. Talk about other objects which need to be carried carefully, such as scissors. (PS1, 9)

COMMUNICATION, LANGUAGE AND LITERACY

- Begin a word bank of words that rhyme with 'ill'. Make lotto games with the words children suggest and enjoy playing lotto. (L11, 13)

- Make up new versions of 'Jack and Jill' by changing the names and the places the children went to. (L1, 3)

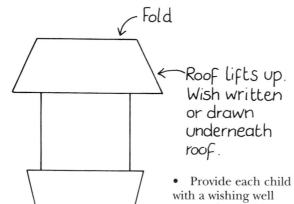

Fold

Roof lifts up. Wish written or drawn underneath roof.

- Provide each child with a wishing well cut out from a piece of A4 folded card (see diagram). Talk about wells as a place where water can be found and also as somewhere where people make wishes. Help children to write their names on the wells, decorate them and write or draw a picture of their wishes under the roof flap. (L16, 17, 18)

MATHEMATICAL DEVELOPMENT

- Use water to estimate, to measure and to compare the capacity of a variety of buckets. (M12)

- When playing with sand, make hills and 'walk' plastic toys up and down them. Encourage children to use the words 'up' and 'down' and to enact the rhyme of 'Jack and Jill'. (M10)

- Jack and Jill are names which have four letters in them. Sort the names of children in the group according to the number of letters that they have in them (see activity opposite). (M2, 4)

- Sort and name 3-d shapes ready for investigating how they move down a hill. (M9)

KNOWLEDGE AND UNDERSTANDING OF THE WORLD

- Investigate the way 3-d shapes move down a hill (see activity opposite). (K1, 4)

- Enjoy investigating the way water behaves as it is poured through funnels, tubes and sieves. (K1)

- Use pictures of countries which have suffered from drought to talk about the importance of not wasting water. Help children to make water-saving posters to remind people to turn off taps. (K9)

PHYSICAL DEVELOPMENT

- Use large apparatus to practise climbing up and down. (PD2, 6, 7)

- Enjoy playing with balls and beanbags. Encourage children to talk about throwing balls and beanbags 'up' and catching them as they drop 'down'. (PD6)

- Practise aiming at targets by throwing beanbags into buckets. (PD6)

CREATIVE DEVELOPMENT

- Make wishing wells from boxes and plastic drinking cups. (C1, 4)

- Use tuned and untuned percussion to make music for the walk of Jack and Jill as they travel up and down the hill. (C5)

- Make puppets of Jack and Jill by decorating wooden spoons. Use the puppets during the singing of the nursery rhyme and to accompany the Jack and Jill percussion music. (C5)

ACTIVITY: Letters in a name

Learning opportunity: Recognising names, counting letters in names and sorting names according to the number of letters in them.

Early Learning Goal: Mathematical Development. Children will count reliably up to ten everyday objects. They will use language such as 'more' or 'less' to compare two numbers.

Resources: Large strips of card on which Jack, Jill and the names of children in the group are written; digit cards showing the numbers from one to ten; large hoops.

Key vocabulary: Numbers one to ten, names of children in the group, more, fewer, how many, count, similar, same.

Organisation: Small group sitting comfortably on the floor.

WHAT TO DO:

As a group, say the rhyme 'Jack and Jill'. Show children the name strips on which Jack and Jill are written. Help the children to read the names. Does anyone notice anything similar about the two names? Children are likely to notice that both names begin with 'j'.

Ask the children to count how many letters there are in the name 'Jill' and then repeat for 'Jack'. Explain that the group is going to sort names according to how many letters they have in them. Place the group's names in a pile in the centre of the group and invite children to find their own name. Does anyone think that their name has the same number of letters as Jack's? Encourage children to count the letters in their names. Sort the names into hoops. Which hoop has the most names? Which hoop has the fewest?

ACTIVITY: Investigating shapes

Learning opportunity: Observing the way cones, balls, cylinders and cubes move down a slope.

Early Learning Goal: Knowledge and Understanding of the World. Children will investigate objects using their senses as appropriate and will ask questions about why things happen.

Resources: A selection of 3-d shapes such as cylinders, cubes, cones and spheres; a safe ramp (hill).

Key vocabulary: Cylinder, cone, cube, ball, round, flat, roll, slide, slip, straight.

Organisation: Small group on the floor.

WHAT TO DO:

Introduce children to the hill and the 3-d shapes. Ask whether they know the names of any of the shapes. During the activity, encourage children to use the correct names. Pick up a sphere. Ask children what they think will happen if it is placed at the top of the hill. Choose a child to release the sphere and to describe what happens as it rolls in a straight line. Repeat this with the other shapes, encouraging children to predict what will happen before testing out their ideas. Help children to notice that some shapes will slide and roll depending upon how they are placed on the hill.

DISPLAY

Divide a large board into sections and label each from one to ten. Give each child a strip of card with their name written on it and ask them to stick it in the section according to the number of letters in their name. On a table, display the model wells and nearby put up the card wishing wells. Ensure that the card wells are at a height where children can easily lift the roof to look at the wish inside.

Week 4

THE GRAND OLD DUKE OF YORK

PERSONAL, SOCIAL AND EMOTIONAL DEVELOPMENT

- As a group, act out 'The Grand Old Duke of York'. Encourage children to take it in turns to be the duke. (PS8)

- Make a collection of postcards which show views of hills, mountains, lakes and other scenes. Discuss which views children like the best and the reasons for their choices. What might the duke have seen when he reached the top of his hill? (PS2, 3)

- Play 'Snakes and ladders'. Encourage children to use the words 'up' and 'down' as they travel along the snakes and ladders. Before the game, talk about the rules for the game. (PS8)

COMMUNICATION, LANGUAGE AND LITERACY

- Read *The Hill and the Rock* by David McKee (Andersen Press). Discuss why Mrs Quest is so fond of her house on the hill and why visitors climb the hill. Help the children to imagine that they have climbed the hill and to make postcards as if bought from Mrs Quest. (L3, 16)

- Make new versions of 'The Grand Old Duke of York'. Read other versions of nursery rhymes, such as those in *Nonsense Nursery Rhymes* by Richard Edwards and Chris Fisher (Oxford University Press), to help children to realise that by changing just a few words, a new rhyme can be made. For example:

    The Grand Old Duke of York,

    He had ten thousand socks,

    He sorted them into their pairs,

    And put them in a box! (L3)

MATHEMATICAL DEVELOPMENT

- The Grand Old Duke had 'ten thousand men'. Talk to children about the number 1,000. Explain that it is a large number and that the duke had ten lots of that large number. Invite children to make collections of ten objects such as ten packets of crayons. (M2)

- Read *One, Two, Three, Oops!* by Michael Coleman and Gwyneth Williamson (Magi Publications). In this book, a father rabbit uses a variety of methods to count his ten children. Encourage children to join in with the counting of the rabbits and the phrases which are repeated throughout the tale. (M2)

- Use playdough to make hills. Encourage children to describe their hills and to compare the height with their friends. Use toy people to climb the hills and to reinforce positional language. (M10, 12)

- Recite 'The Grand Old Duke of York' and discuss what is meant by 'half way up'. Provide each child with a brightly coloured strip of paper. Show them how the strips can be folded and cut so that they have two pieces which are halves. Use the strips to make a group flag for the duke. (M12)

KNOWLEDGE AND UNDERSTANDING OF THE WORLD

- Make drums for a Grand Old Duke of York parade (see activity opposite). (K1, 3)

- In order to see all of his men, the duke probably would have had to use binoculars or a telescope. Talk about instruments which can be used to help us see over long distances. Make a collection of toy binoculars and telescopes for children to enjoy playing with. Remind children not to look at the sun. (K1)

- Make model binoculars and telescopes from cardboard tubes. (K5, 6)

PHYSICAL DEVELOPMENT

- Play 'Follow my leader' in which the leader is the Duke of York. (PD1, 2)

- Repeat the activities carried out on large apparatus during the 'Jack and Jill week' to reinforce climbing 'up' and 'down'. (PD2, 6, 7)

CREATIVE DEVELOPMENT

- Paint portraits to display on a large frieze of a hill. Help children to select colours which match their eyes, skin and hair (see activity opposite). (C1, 4)

- Use pastel crayons to make hilly scenes. Show children how to smudge the colours with a tissue

to make interesting landscapes. (C1, 4)

- In *The Hill and the Rock* by David McKee, Mr Quest paints a scene on the large rock. Use ready-mixed paints and thin brushes to paint large pebbles. Some children may wish to try and paint a scene whilst others may simply enjoy painting patterns. (C1)

ACTIVITY: Making drums

Learning opportunity: Comparing sounds and making drums.

Early Learning Goal: Knowledge and Understanding of the World. Children will investigate objects by using all of their senses as appropriate and they will look closely at similarities and differences.

Resources: A small drum; a variety of clean boxes, tins and plastic pots; pieces of dowel about 15 cm long; scraps of shiny paper; glue; picture of a parade with people drumming.

Key vocabulary: Drum, loud, quiet, quick, slow, tap, beat.

Organisation: Small group.

WHAT TO DO:

Show children the picture of the parade. Explain that when the Grand Old Duke marched his many men, there were probably drummers to keep the men in time.

Show children the drum. Ask one child to tap it quietly three times. Ask another to tap it slowly four times. Finally, ask a third child to tap it loudly and then softly. Talk about the different sounds that the children made and how a drum can be played both quietly and loudly.

Show children the range of resources available for them to make a drum. Help the children to investigate the different sounds which can be made by beating with a dowel or tapping with a hand. Help them to compare the sounds made by a tin, a box and a pot. Invite each child to select one container for their drum and to decorate the sides with scraps of shiny paper.

ACTIVITY: Painting self-portraits

Learning opportunity: Painting based on close observation.

Early Learning Goal: Creative Development. Children will explore colour and shape in two dimensions. They will use their imagination in art.

Resources: Plastic mirrors; ready-mixed paints in a variety of colours to allow children to be able to select their appropriate skin, eye and hair colours; A3 sized paper; display board with a background of a large hill.

Key vocabulary: Portrait, names for parts of the body and colours.

Organisation: Small group.

WHAT TO DO:

Show the display board with the hill background. Explain that everyone is going to paint a picture of themselves. Encourage children to look in the mirrors and to describe their eye, hair and skin colours. Show the children the available paints and ask them to select the ones they are likely to need. Talk about the types of clothes that they would wear if they were going to march to the top of a hill. Help the group to paint their own portraits. Talk about the word portrait. When dry, cut out the portraits and invite children to suggest where they would like their portraits to be placed. Encourage them to describe the positions in which their portraits are stuck.

DISPLAY

On a large board, make a background of a large hill for the children's portraits. On another board, display the pastel scenes and on a nearby table place the painted pebbles and *The Hill and the Rock* by David McKee. On a label, invite children to select the view that they think Mrs Quest would like to have painted on her rock.

Week 5

HICKORY, DICKORY, DOCK

PERSONAL, SOCIAL AND EMOTIONAL DEVELOPMENT

- In 'Hickory, Dickory, Dock', the mouse runs when it hears the clock strike. Discuss with children the sounds which can frighten people and animals and also those which are useful, such as ambulance sirens. (PS2)

- During a circle time, use a minute sand timer to give children a feeling of a minute. Discuss what can be achieved in a minute, such as fastening a shoe or doing five jumps. Challenge children to complete a variety of simple tasks within a minute. Pass the sand timer around the circle and invite children to finish the sentence 'In one minute I can...'. Only the child holding the timer is allowed to speak. Children who do not wish to speak just pass the timer on. (PS1, 2, 3)

- Tell or read a version of Aesop's fable of 'The Hare and the Tortoise'. Talk about the hare who did not use his time wisely and simply went to sleep. (PS3, 9, 12)

COMMUNICATION, LANGUAGE AND LITERACY

- As a group, write a counting rhyme based on 'Hickory, Dickory, Dock' (see activity opposite). (L3)

- Make a collection of words that rhyme with 'tick' and ones that rhyme with 'tock'. Either scribe the words for children to illustrate or encourage them to write the words. Help children to notice how important the 'i' and 'o' are for changing the way the word sounds. (L11, 12)

- As a group, make up a story about the mouse. Where did it go after it ran down the clock? Where did it live? Make a big book of 'The tale of Hickory, Dickory, Dock's mouse'. (L3)

MATHEMATICAL DEVELOPMENT

- Make a collection of clocks and watches cut from magazines and catalogues. Encourage children to sort them according to the shape of the faces. (M9)

- Enjoy reciting the group's counting rhyme based on 'Hickory, Dickory, Dock'. Encourage children to clap for each verse the number of times the clock struck. (M2)

- Use a large model clock face to introduce children to o'clock times. The times used will depend upon the numerals which individual children are able to recognise. (M3)

- Enjoy playing with plastic sand timers. Talk about 'more' and 'less' time. (M12)

KNOWLEDGE AND UNDERSTANDING OF THE WORLD

- Enjoy making grandfather clocks from cardboard boxes, paper plates and hands attached with brass fasteners. (K5, 6)

- Investigate which materials magnets will attract. Make mice from card covered with felt or fur fabric. Stick a small magnet on the reverse side of the mouse and steel paper-clips on parts of the clocks. The mouse can then 'walk' up and down the clock as it is attracted to the clips. (K1, 5)

PHYSICAL DEVELOPMENT

- Outside, use playground chalk to make a large clock face. Play games in which children are mice that move to different numbers. Encourage children to listen carefully to instructions and to move in ways as described. (PD1, 2, 3)

- Play a game in which children move according to the number of times that a triangle is struck, such as 1 strike = jump on the spot; 2 strikes = stand still; 3 strikes = skip, and so on. (PD1, 2, 3)

- Make mice from playdough or clay. Experiment with a variety of plastic objects to see what can be used to give the mouse texture or a furry appearance. (PD8)

CREATIVE DEVELOPMENT

- Provide each child with a large circle of paper. Ask children to paint a picture of a particular time on the circle (for example, bed time, night time, tea time, half time). Mount the circles on silhouettes of clocks cut from black sugar paper (see activity opposite). (C4)

- Use a variety of untuned percussion instruments to provide an accompaniment for the reciting of 'Hickory, Dickory, Dock'. (C2)

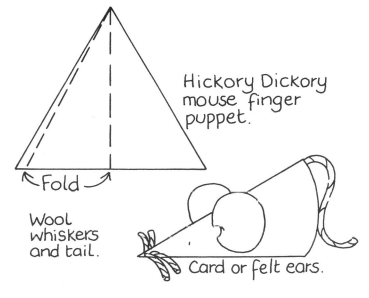

Hickory Dickory
mouse finger
puppet.

Fold

Wool
whiskers
and tail.

Card or felt ears.

- Use triangles of card folded in half to make finger puppet mice (see diagram). Use the puppets to provide actions during the singing of 'Hickory, Dickory, Dock'. (C2)

ACTIVITY: Writing a counting rhyme

Learning opportunity: Collaborating to make a counting rhyme.

Early Learning Goal: Communication, Language and Literacy. Children will be able to listen with enjoyment and respond to rhymes and to make up their own rhymes.

Resources: Flip chart; big book version of 'Hickory, Dickory, Dock'.

Key vocabulary: Numbers to ten.

Organisation: Small group.

WHAT TO DO:

As a group, enjoy reciting familiar number rhymes. Look together at the big book version of 'Hickory, Dickory, Dock'. What time did the clock strike? Explain that together the group is going to write a new rhyme in which the clock strikes first one, then two, then three and so on. Together, brainstorm words which rhyme with each of the numbers from one to ten. Help the children to think of new rhyming couplets for each number and scribe their ideas. Finally, scribe the complete poem and invite each child to illustrate their own verse.

Example rhymes:

Hickory, Dickory, Dock,
The mouse ran up the clock,
The clock struck two
The mouse shouted 'Boo!'
Hickory, Dickory, Dock.   *(Jonathan, aged 4)*
The clock struck eight
The mouse squeaked 'I'm late!'   *(Alice, aged 5)*

ACTIVITY: Making clock time pictures

Learning opportunity: Drawing and colouring pictures to show a time of day.

Early Learning Goal: Creative Development. Children will be able to use their imaginations in art.

Resources: Circles cut from white paper; silhouettes of clocks cut from black sugar paper; variety of crayons and felt-pens.

Key vocabulary: Time, clock face.

Organisation: Small group.

WHAT TO DO:

Show the children the silhouettes of clocks. Do they know what they are? Can anyone find a grandfather clock? Is there a cuckoo clock? Invite each child to select one clock. Give each child a circle and ask them to place it on the silhouette for a clock face. Describe some times of day and ask children to guess which time it is. Describe breakfast time, play time, night time and so on. Ask children to choose a time and to draw and colour a picture of it on the clock face. Stick the faces on the clocks and display them.

DISPLAY

Cover a large noticeboard with a simple patterned or plain wallpaper and use this as a background for the silhouette clocks. On labels, write out the times which the clocks depict and invite children to match the labels with their clocks. Arrange the model clocks nearby along with the dough and clay mice. Ask children to make 'Please do not touch' labels to go with their models.

Week 6

LITTLE BO PEEP AND THE NURSERY RHYME DAY

PERSONAL, SOCIAL AND EMOTIONAL DEVELOPMENT

- Little Bo Peep lost her sheep. Discuss how it feels to lose something and the joy when something lost is found. (PS2)

- Talk about the importance of looking after clothes and toys. Decorate clothes pegs for keeping pairs of wellington boots together. (PS9)

- Talk about the preparations for the nursery rhyme day. (PS2, 3)

COMMUNICATION, LANGUAGE AND LITERACY

- Make 'Lost sheep' posters for Little Bo Peep. (L16)

- Read stories which have sheep as central characters such as *Friska, the Sheep that was too Small* by Rob Lewis (Macdonald Young Books). Later in the week, encourage children to retell the stories. (L3, 6, 9)

- Make a 'phonic die' from a cube-shaped box. Write 'sh', 'p', 'd', 'k' and 'w' on five of the sides and leave the sixth face blank. On a second cube, write 'eep'. Encourage children to take turns to throw the letter die, to place it in front of 'eep' and to say the word they have made. As children become more confident, other letter patterns introduced through previous weeks' nursery rhymes can be written on dice. (L13)

MATHEMATICAL DEVELOPMENT

- Use card sheep with numbers printed on them to reinforce the recognition and ordering of numerals. Invite the children to arrange the sheep in numerical order. Ask the children to close their eyes. Remove a sheep. Do the children know which one is missing? (M2, 3)

- Enjoy using the 'Little Bo Peep' counting rhyme to introduce and reinforce number bonds to ten (see activity opposite). (M2, 11)

- Use toy sheep to reinforce positional language. Place a number of sheep around the room. Explain that Bo Peep's sheep are hiding in the room. Invite children to find the sheep and to describe where they are hiding. On another occasion, invite a child to hide a sheep and to describe where it is so that others may find it. (M10)

KNOWLEDGE AND UNDERSTANDING OF THE WORLD

- Talk about what wool is used for. Explain how wool comes from sheep and tell the story of a woollen jumper from sheep to spinning, to knitting, to jumper. (K1, 2, 4)

- Make a display of pictures of sheep and things made from wool. Invite children to bring in contributions for the display and to write or trace over their own name labels. Help children to look closely at the things in their display and to compare the similarities and differences in the items made from wool. (K3)

- Shepherds often give sheep marks, letters or numbers so that they can be identified. Talk about colours which can be seen easily and how Little Bo Peep might have been unable to find her sheep because she could not recognise them as her own. Invite children to make labels for Little Bo Peep. (K9)

PHYSICAL DEVELOPMENT

- Use a range of balancing and climbing equipment for children to travel on as they pretend to be Little Bo Peep's sheep journeying home. (PD7)

- Make sheep from cornflour dough. (PD8)

- Shepherds use sheep dogs to help round up sheep. Play a chasing game in which one child is the dog who has to catch his or her sheep. Once a sheep is caught, it moves to the side. Encourage children to move safely, looking out for others. Invite a number of children to take it in turns to be the dog and after each go, count the number of sheep that have been caught. (PD1, 2, 3)

CREATIVE DEVELOPMENT

- Use cotton wool balls to make collage pictures of Little Bo Peep's sheep. (C1)

- Make woven sheep with wool (see activity below). (C1)

- Paint portraits of how the children hope to dress on the nursery rhyme day. (C4)

ACTIVITY: Using the Bo Peep counting rhyme

Learning opportunity: Joining in a counting rhyme to reinforce numbers to ten and language involved in adding and subtracting.

Early Learning Goal: Mathematical Development. Children will be able to count reliably up to ten everyday objects and begin to use the language involved in adding and subtracting.

brass fastener
wool
slits cut out.

Resources: None.

Key vocabulary: Numbers from one to ten; how many more?

Organisation: Whole group sitting comfortably on the floor.

WHAT TO DO:

Talk to the children about Little Bo Peep and her lost sheep. She probably counted them many times to check how many were missing. Teach the group the

Little Bo Peep counting rhyme below. After the first verse, choose a child to be a sheep and continue the rhyme until Bo Peep has ten sheep. On further occasions, the line 'That means there is/are ____ more to find!' can be added to encourage children to think about how many sheep are missing if Little Bo Peep's flock has ten sheep in it.

Little Bo Peep has lots of sheep,
She counts them every day.
She likes it when,
She gets to ten
And all are safe away.
Let's help her count (count the sheep)
(Insert number) sheep!

ACTIVITY: Weaving sheep

Learning opportunity: Weaving with a variety of yarns and colours.

Early Learning Goal: Creative Development. Children will be able to explore colour and texture in two dimensions.

Resources: A wide range of different coloured wools; card sheep with precut slits for weaving (see diagram).

Key vocabulary: Sheep, wool, weave, in, out.

Organisation: Small group.

WHAT TO DO:

Provide each child with a sheep for weaving. Talk to children about wool and where it comes from. Show children the different colours of wool available. Encourage them to describe the textures of the different wools and to talk about their favourite colours.

Show the group how to cut a piece of wool, tape it on the back of the sheep and weave it through the slits.

To produce a sheep with a nodding head, cut the sheep's head separately and attach it to the body with a brass fastener after the weaving has been finished.

DISPLAY

Prepare a large noticeboard with a background of grass and blue sky. Arrange the woven sheep in the field. Cover a nearby table with green cloth and arrange the cornflour dough sheep.

BRINGING IT ALL TOGETHER

THE NURSERY RHYME DAY

Explain to the children that they are going to have a special day on which anyone who wants to can dress up as a nursery rhyme character. Part of the day will be spent repeating favourite nursery rhyme activities carried out during the topic and selected by the children. Together make lists of all the activities children would like to try again and characters children would like to dress up as. Recite the rhymes. Talk about the kinds of clothes which each character might wish to wear. Explain that parents and friends will be invited to come to the event to hear the group recite nursery rhymes, to eat nursery rhyme food and to look at their pictures and models.

PREPARATION

• Nursery rhyme costumes
At the start of the topic, tell parents about the dressing up for the planned nursery rhyme day. Explain that the costumes can be very simple and that children who do not want to dress up might instead wish to choose a nursery rhyme character and bring in a related object. Miss Muffet might, for instance, carry a toy spider. Encourage children to get into role as their chosen character and to look at nursery rhyme books to gain ideas for their costumes.

• Nursery rhyme chest
Invite children to help decorate a large box with a lid. Make a pretend key for the box. Explain to the children that it is a magic chest full of nursery rhymes. On large strips of card, draw a picture and write the titles for the rhymes which children have chosen to dress up for on the Nursery Rhyme Day.

• Nursery rhyme food
Involve the children in inventing and making nursery rhyme food. Humpty Dumpty and webs for Miss Muffet's spider could be made by decorating small circular biscuits with chocolate and icing. Bo Peep's sheep and the three blind mice can be made from fondant icing. Small buns could be decorated as Mary, Mary's flowers.

ACTIVITIES

On the day, set out a large room with a circuit of nursery rhyme activities suggested by the group. Invite additional helpers so that every activity has an adult helper. Make sure that there are spare activities because they will not all take the same length of time. Invite children to lend jigsaw puzzles and games which involve nursery rhyme characters.

The concert
On the nursery rhyme day, present a short concert for

parents and friends. Explain that the magic chest is full of rhymes which will be unlocked for them to enjoy. Invite children in turn to pretend to unlock the chest and to pick a card. Children who have come as a character from the rhyme can then stand to show their costumes and the group can recite or sing the rhyme. To finish the concert, sing 'In nursery rhyme land we can clap' to the tune of 'If you're happy and you know it, clap your hands'. Finally, encourage children to share the nursery rhyme food with their parents and friends.

RESOURCES

RESOURCES TO COLLECT

- Plastic minibeasts (toy shops).
- Pipe-cleaners.
- Sand timers.
- Toy binoculars and telescopes.
- Pictures of parades and spiders' webs.

EVERYDAY RESOURCES

- Glitter.
- Boxes, large and small for modelling.
- Papers and cards of different weights, colours and textures, for example sugar, corrugated card, silver and shiny papers.
- Dry powder paints for mixing and mixed paints for covering large areas such as card tree trunks.
- Different sized paint brushes from household brushes to thin brushes for delicate work and a variety of paint mixing containers.
- A variety of drawing and colouring pencils, crayons, pastels, charcoals, and so on.
- Additional decorative and finishing materials such as sequins, foils, glitter, tinsel, shiny wool and threads, beads, pieces of textiles, parcel ribbon.
- Table covers.
- Cardboard tubes.

STORIES

One, Two, Three, Oops! by Michael Coleman and Gwyneth Williamson (Magi Publications).

Hepzibah's Woolly Fleece by Jill Dow (Frances Lincoln).

The Hare and the Tortoise and other favourite fables retold by Vernon Goldsmith and Helen Kandel Hyman (Ramboro Books).

Dear Bear by Joanna Harrison (Collins Picture Lions).

Little Lumpty by Miko Imai (Walker Books).

Friska and the Sheep that was too Small by Rob Lewis (Macdonald Young Books).

Morag and the Lamb by Joan Lingard and Patricia Casey (Walker Books).

The Hill and the Rock by David McKee (Andersen Press).

NON FICTION

Planning for Learning through Minibeasts by Rachel Sparks Linfield and Penny Coltman (Step Forward Publishing). Useful for more ideas about spider activities.

Minibeasts by Angela Royston (Dorling Kindersley).

Bugs and Slugs by Judy Tatchell (Usborne Publishing).

SONGS

Okki-tokki-unga Action Songs for Children chosen by Beatrice Harrop, Linda Friend and David Gadsby (A & C Black).

Apusskido Songs for Children chosen by Beatrice Harrop, Peggy Blakely and David Gadsby (A & C Black).

POEMS

Incy-Wincy Moo-Cow - A Collection of Weird and Wacky Nursery Rhymes by John Cunliffe (Macdonald Young Books).

Nonsense Nursery Rhymes by Richard Edwards and Chris Fisher (Oxford University Press).

Minibeast Poems compiled by John Foster (Oxford University Press).

Out and About by Shirley Hughes (Walker Books).

This Little Puffin by Elizabeth Matterson (Puffin).

My Big Book compiled by Walker Books.

Pudding and Pie Favourite Nursery Rhymes chosen by Sarah Williams (Oxford University Press).

All books were available from leading booksellers at the time of writing.

COLLECTING EVIDENCE OF CHILDREN'S LEARNING

Monitoring children's development is an important task. Keeping a record of children's achievements will help you to see progress and will draw attention to those who are having difficulties for some reason. If a child needs additional professional help, such as speech therapy, your records will provide valuable evidence.

Records should be the result of collaboration between group leaders, parents and carers. Parents should be made aware of your record keeping policies when their child joins your group. Show them the type of records you are keeping and make sure they understand that they have an opportunity to contribute. As a general rule, your records should form an open document. Any parent should have access to records relating to his or her child. Take regular opportunities to talk to parents about children's progress. If you have formal discussions regarding children about whom you have particular concerns, a dated record of the main points should be kept.

KEEPING IT MANAGEABLE

Records should be helpful in informing group leaders, adult helpers and parents and always be for the benefit of the child. However, keeping records of every aspect of each child's development can become a difficult task. The sample shown will help to keep records manageable and useful. The golden rule is to keep them simple.

Observations will basically fall into three categories:

- **Spontaneous records:** Sometimes you will want to make a note of observations as they happen, for example when a child is heard counting cars accurately during a play activity, or is seen to play collaboratively for the first time.

- **Planned observations:** Sometimes you will plan to make observations of children's developing skills in their everyday activities. Using the learning opportunity identified for an activity will help you to make appropriate judgements about children's capabilities and to record them systematically.

To collect information:

- talk to children about their activities and listen to their responses;

- listen to children talking to each other;

- observe children's work such as early writing, drawings, paintings and 3-d models. (Keeping photocopies or photographs is sometimes useful.)

Sometimes you may wish to set up 'one-off' activities for the purposes of monitoring development. Some groups, for example, ask children to make a drawing of themselves at the beginning of each term to record their progressing skills in both co-ordination and observation. Do not attempt to make records following every activity!

- **Reflective observations:** It is useful to spend regular time reflecting on the progress of a few children (about four children each week). Aim to make some brief comments about each child every half term.

INFORMING YOUR PLANNING

Collecting evidence about children's progress is time-consuming but essential. When you are planning, use the information you have collected to help you to decide what learning opportunities you need to provide next for children. For example, a child who has poor pencil or brush control will benefit from more play with dough or construction toys to build the strength of hand muscles.

Example of recording chart

Name: Jonathan Hogg			D.O.B. 18.2.97		Date of entry: 13.9.00	
Term	**Personal, Social and Emotional**	**Communication, Language and Literacy**	**Mathematical Development**	**Knowledge and Understanding of the World**	**Physical Development**	**Creative Development**
ONE	Reluctant to say good-bye to mother. Prefers adult company. **20.9.00 EMH**	Enjoys listening to and reciting nursery rhymes. 'Humpty Dumpty' is a particular favourite. Can write first name. Good pencil grip. **20.10.00 EMH**	Is able to say numbers up to ten and count accurately five objects. Recognises sphere and circle. **5.11.00 EHL**	Eager to ask questions. Fascinated by the web experiment. **16.10.00 LSS**	Can balance on one leg. Loves climbing on the big apparatus. Does not like the feel of playdough **16.10.00 AC**	Enjoys painting, particularly mixing own colours. **16.10.00 EHL**
TWO						
THREE						

SKILLS OVERVIEW OF SIX-WEEK PLAN

Week	Topic focus	Personal, Social and Emotional Development	Communication, Language and Literacy	Mathematical Development	Knowledge and Understanding of the World	Physical Development	Creative Development
1	Humpty Dumpty	Listening Expressing emotions	Rhyming Listening Writing Recognising initial sounds	Recognising numbers Estimating Counting	Making observations Comparing Describing	Moving with control and imagination Using malleable materials	Role play Collage Painting
2	Little Miss Muffet	Listening Taking turns Developing independence	Rhyming Listening Writing, Recognising initial sounds	Counting Awareness of 2-d shapes	Making observations Comparing, Describing	Moving with control and imagination	Painting Using materials
3	Jack and Jill	Sensitivity to others Safety awareness Listening	Listening to stories Recognising initial sounds Rhyming	Comparative language Positional language Recognising 3-d shapes	Comparing similarities and differences, Observing	Moving with control and imagination, Throwing, Aiming	Making sounds Making models, Making and using puppets
4	The Grand Old Duke of York	Taking turns Listening	Using descriptive vocabulary, Rhyming Talking	Comparative language Counting	Talking Observing Investigating	Moving with control and awareness of space	Using materials Making sounds Making models
5	Hickory, Dickory, Dock	Expressing emotions	Rhyming Discussing	Counting Recognising 2-d shapes Telling o'clock times	Investigating materials	Moving with control Using malleable materials	Playing instruments Painting
6	Little Bo Peep and the Nursery Rhyme Day	Expressing emotions Collaborative planning	Listening to a story Writing for a purpose Recognising initial sounds	Recognising numbers Counting Positional language	Observing Describing Investigating Comparing	Moving with imagination, control and awareness of space Using malleable materials	Collage Weaving Painting

HOME LINKS

The theme of Nursery Rhymes lends itself to useful links with children's homes and families. Through working together, children and adults gain respect for each other and build comfortable and confident relationships.

ESTABLISHING PARTNERSHIPS

- Keep parents informed about the topic of Nursery Rhymes and the themes for each week. By understanding the work of the group, parents will enjoy the involvement of contributing ideas, time and resources.

- Photocopy the parent's page for each child to take home.

- Invite friends, childminders and families to share all or part of the nursery rhyme day.

VISITING ENTHUSIASTS

- Invite adults to come to the group to talk about their favourite nursery rhymes and to read and recite rhymes from their own childhood.

RESOURCE REQUESTS

- Ask parents to contribute clothes and artefacts for role play as nursery rhyme characters and games and puzzles that depict nursery rhyme characters.

- Fabrics, shiny paper, ribbon and wool scraps are invaluable for collage work and a wide range of interesting activities. Many wallpapers, wrapping papers, curtain fabrics and birthday cards feature nursery rhymes.

THE NURSERY RHYME DAY

- Explain to parents that the costumes for the nursery rhyme day can be simple and encourage them to let their children do as much of their own preparation for them as is possible.

- It is always useful to have extra adults at times such as the nursery rhyme day. Invite parents and other carers to come in and help.

- Put out a suggestion book in which parents can write down nursery rhyme foods that they are willing to provide for the day.